The ESCAPE MANUAL for Introverts

Also by Katie Vaz

Don't Worry, Eat Cake
Make Yourself Cozy

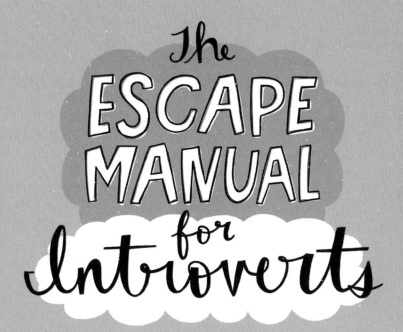

The ESCAPE MANUAL for Introverts

Katie Vaz

Andrews McMeel
PUBLISHING®

Andrews McMeel Publishing
a division of Andrews McMeel Universal
1130 Walnut Street, Kansas City, Missouri 64106

www.andrewsmcmeel.com

19 20 21 22 23 TEN 10 9 8 7 6 5 4 3 2 1

ISBN: 978-1-4494-9369-1

Library of Congress Control Number: 2018966056

Editor: Patty Rice
Art Director: Diane Marsh
Production Editor: Amy Strassner
Production Manager: Tamara Haus

ATTENTION: SCHOOLS AND BUSINESSES
Andrews McMeel books are available at quantity discounts with bulk purchase for educational, business, or sales promotional use. For information, please e-mail the Andrews McMeel Publishing Special Sales Department: specialsales@amuniversal.com.

For my mom, for everything

JUST BECAUSE
I DON'T
WANT TO GO
doesn't mean
I DON'T
like you.

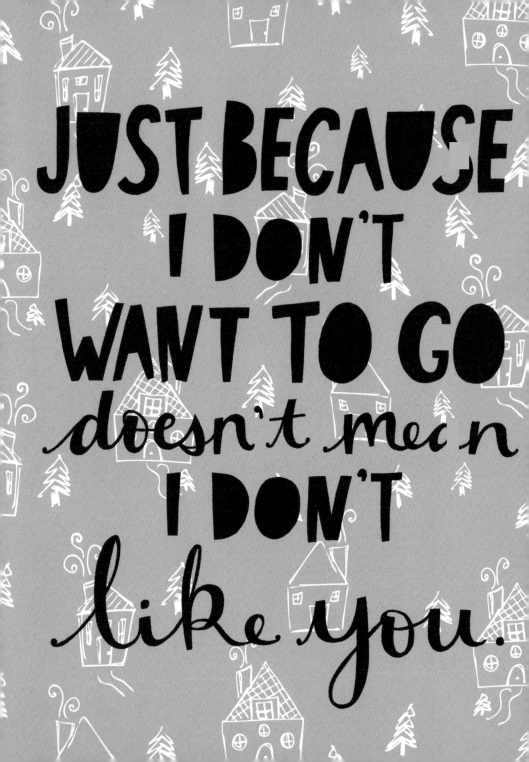

To the fellow introvert

An extra amount of solitude is necessary for introverts to feel sane, yet finding ways to explain that to extroverts can be tricky. Just because we don't want to go doesn't mean we don't like them, but that can be hard to get across kindly. As an introvert myself, I know how easy it is to get pulled into social situations if a proper excuse isn't prepared ahead of time. Once you're out, it's just as easy to stay out longer than desired if a clever departure hasn't been planned. How unfortunate it is to find yourself cornered in a sea of extroverts unexpectedly and be at a loss for how to flee.

I created this handbook to be a cheeky illustrated guide to strengthen your arsenal of cover stories for when "I just want to be home" isn't going to cut it. In addition to authentically plausible alibis, you'll also find a catalog of exit strategies and preparation plans for protection in various future social situations you may find yourself stuck in. These range from simple and practical all the way to positively preposterous and ingenious! Not only applicable to introverts, folks who identify as socially awkward may find these expert evasions useful as well.

The situations in this book are inspired by all the common scenarios I've found myself trapped in, as well as by the stories my introverted friends and I have shared about past unsuccessful social exits. I hope this collection is useful to you in your journey of navigating an introverted life. With this manual in your repertoire, the days of amateur social-escape artistry are behind you.

How to use this book

Different levels of relation require particular amounts of realism, and this book uniquely tailors to each one. It's divided into five chapters of familiarity: FRIENDS, RELATIVES, COWORKERS, ACQUAINTANCES, and STRANGERS. Within each chapter are examples of social scenarios common to that type of relationship, followed by a selection of escapes and excuses for introverts to use in the moment or as a plan of attack for future encounters.

Use this "Plausibility of Excuse Absurdity" graph as a guideline to how eccentric your escape can safely be to maintain reasonable amounts of believability. Situations involving friends can be delicate and may require more carefully constructed strategies to protect the friendship. Situations with strangers, however, can greatly benefit from deliberate and resourceful tomfoolery.

Peruse the manual at leisure, or flip to any familiarity chapter as needed and according to the social situations you are experiencing or expect to soon.

For your reference, each chapter can quickly be located by the page numbers below.

the PLAUSIBILITY OF EXCUSE ABSURDITY graph

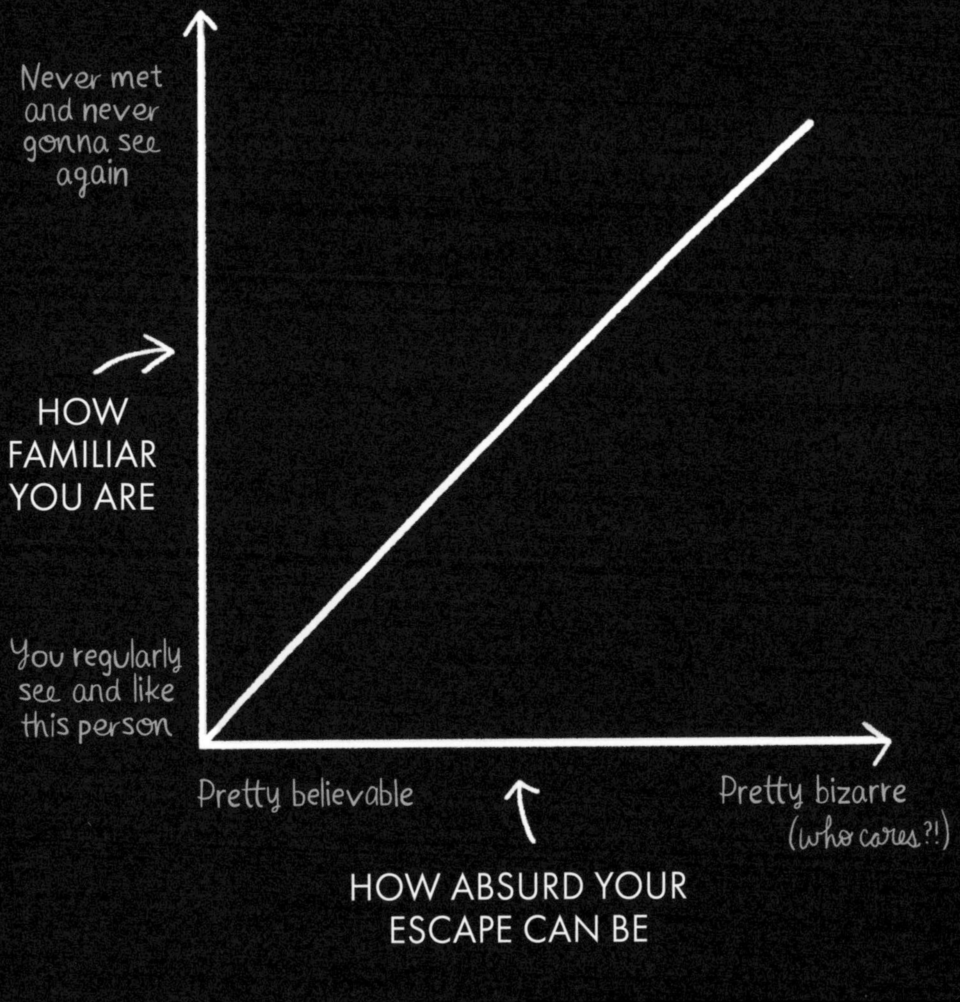

Chapter 1

FRIENDS

How to keep friend hangouts to a reasonable amount (and still keep your friends)

Good friends will understand your introverted ways, so the escapes and excuses in this chapter should be used carefully!

Oh, that tricky balance between sweet alone time and seeing people you like.

Scenario 1

FRIENDS WHO LOVE TRIVIA NIGHT AND WANT YOU TO COME WITH THEM

"I already made plans with _____."

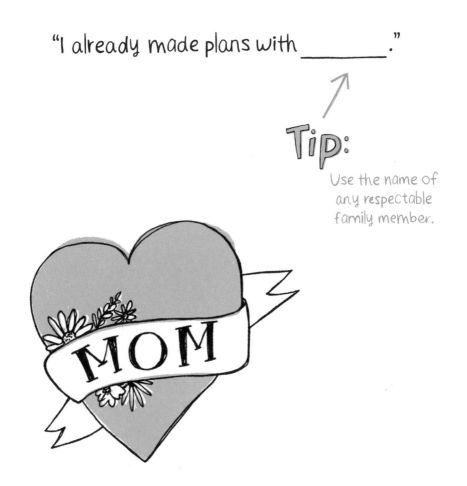

Tip:
Use the name of any respectable family member.

Use partner's name, child's name, pet's name, etc.

"_____ has been feeling neglected lately."

Tip:

This is more likely to be understood by people with pets, children, or needy partners.

Compromise by going once.

Make sure to answer quickly and incorrectly a couple of times to reduce frequency of future invitations.

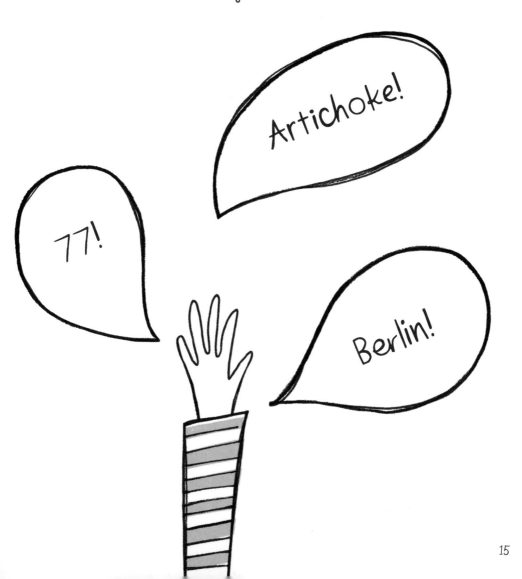

Scenario 2

A RAMBUNCTIOUS DINNER PARTY WITH TOO MANY PEOPLE

Become preoccupied playing with the animals.

Speak quietly and murmur to encourage the surrender of the conversation.

After they give up or resort to smiling and nodding, you can probably say whatever you want.

Keep asking questions that
require long responses.

It means less speaking time for you.
You're probably already a good listener anyway.

Scenario 3

HANGOUTS ARE ALWAYS BIG GROUP ACTIVITIES

"I can't tonight. Could we reschedule to a craft night on _____?"

Tip: You should actually follow through on this if you like this friend.

Bonus points if you suggest an introvert-friendly activity.

If you must go, locate another
introvert in the group.

Become absorbed in a quiet conversation with them,
as per usual introvert style.

Suggest very specific activities for future hangouts.

Pick ones that you think only one or two friends might take you up on.

Canning 101 class

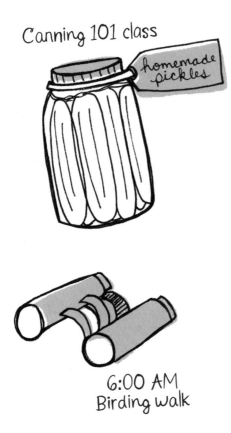

homemade pickles

Hot yoga

6:00 AM
Birding walk

Scenario 4

A PHONE CALL FROM SOMEONE YOU GENUINELY LIKE BUT DON'T WANT TO TALK ON THE PHONE TO

INCOMING CALL...

"I'm actually expecting a call
from _____."

Fill in with anything that sounds official or important.

Tip:

Offer a replacement for the
phone conversation, perhaps by
inviting this person over soon.

pretty fast
INTERNET

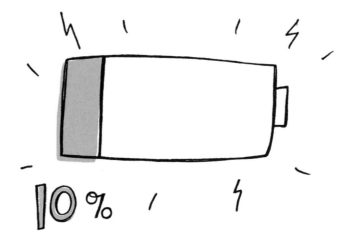

"Whoops, I think my battery
is about to die."

Kindly wrap up the conversation and be careful
not to imply for them to try again later.

Answer the phone in a whisper
and say, "_____ is napping."

Suggest a quiet alternative like texting.

Tip: Use your roommate's
name, pet's name, etc.

Scenario 5

A GAME NIGHT THAT IS LASTING LONGER THAN YOU'D LIKE

Bribe a confidant to stealthily flip the circuit breaker.

Do not be prepared with candles.

Turn off the music very pointedly
at the desired time.

Start the yawning train.

Scenario 6

NOT ENOUGH ALONE TIME WHILE LIVING WITH AN OUTGOING ROOMMATE

Take note of whether they're a
morning or night person. Be the opposite.

When they want to invite people over,
offer to make food or drinks.

Tasks like this can keep you busy to avoid dreaded small talk.

Schedule weekly dates to spend organized, quality time together.

Feel less guilty for all the other days you keep to yourself.

Chapter 2

RELATIVES

How to get out of excess family bonding

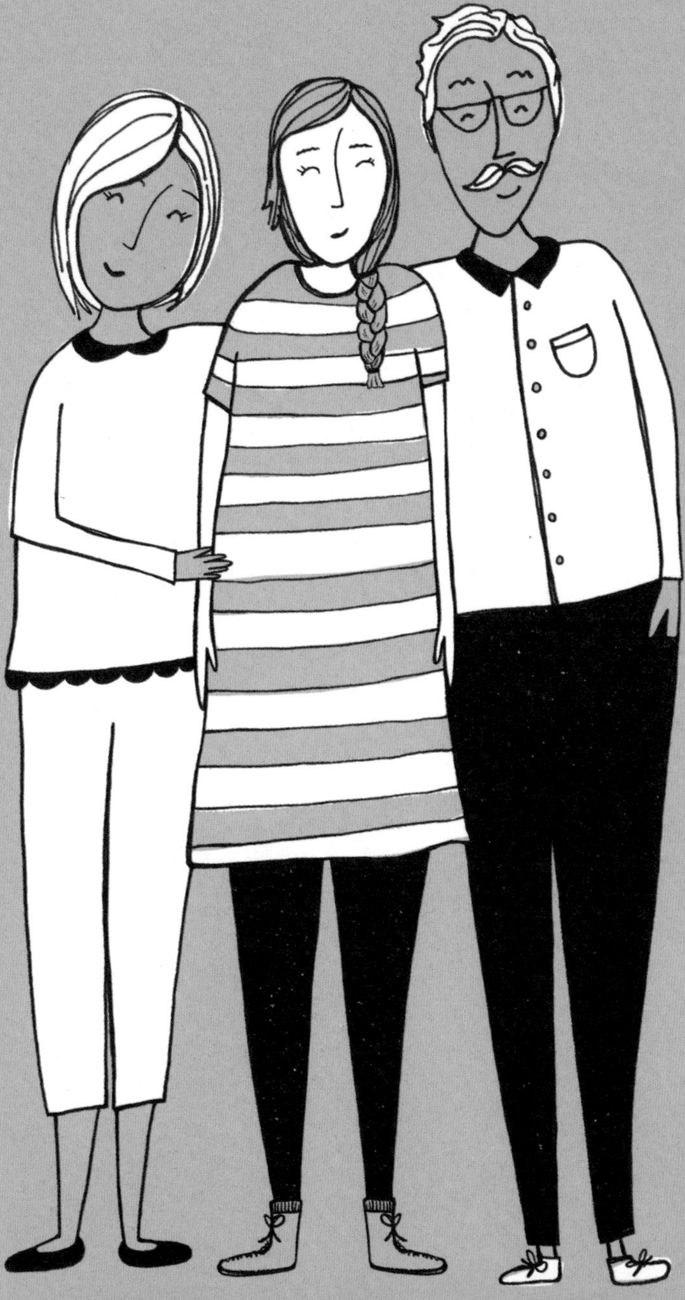

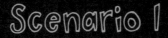

Scenario 1

A FAMILY REUNION THAT
DOESN'T SEEM TO HAVE AN END TIME

Tip: Bring something like lasagna with you to make this excuse appear more legitimate.

"I should head home to clean my oven—
something spilled earlier."

Who could argue with fire safety?

Have a pet that "requires" frequent check-ins.

"Oh no! I think I left my _____ on!"

Tip:
Fill in with an appliance
found in your home.

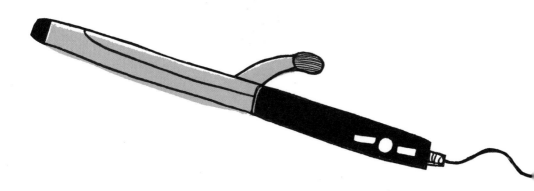

Scenario 2

BEING SURROUNDED BY CHATTY WEDDING GUESTS AT YOUR COUSIN'S NUPTIALS

Slip away to request songs with the DJ.

Maybe you do really care about everyone
having a good time dancing.

"The bride needs me."

Dare anyone to question the bride.

"I'd better go sign the guest book
before I ~~forget~~!"

Scenario 3

A BIG ACTIVITY-PACKED EXTENDED FAMILY VACATION

Call ahead and request a room change.

Request one that is far, far away from the rest of your party.

Pack fitness clothes and steal
yourself away each day to go "work out."

That could totally mean sitting
quietly by yourself somewhere secret to recharge.

X-RAY VISION

JOURNAL

PRETZELS

Pack a compact pop-up privacy
tent in your suitcase.

Zip yourself into it when needed.

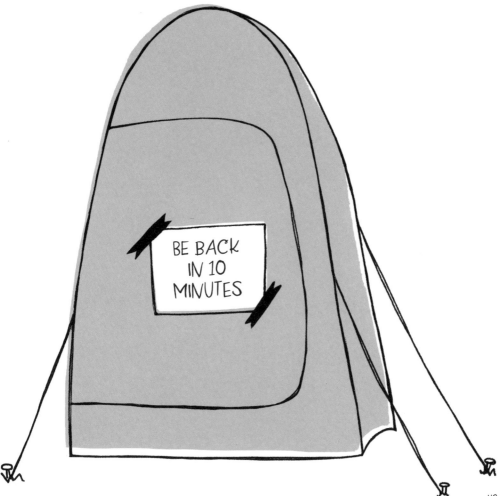

WHEN SAYING GOODBYE AFTER A FAMILY GATHERING DRAGS ON AND ON AND ON . . .

Tip: Schedule things like dental cleanings, eye exams, haircuts, acupuncture, etc.

SATURDAY august 10, 2019

7:00 AM
8:00 AM
9:00 AM — yoga class
10:00 AM
11:00 AM
12:00 PM
1:00 PM — lunch at aunt carla's
2:00 PM — Haircut
3:00 PM
4:00 PM
5:00 PM
6:00 PM
7:00 PM
8:00 PM
9:00 PM

Schedule important appointments directly after gatherings.

You can choose exactly how long you'll stay.

"dog, cat, fish, succulent, etc."

"My _____ has anxiety and can't be left alone for too long."

Become skilled at walking backward smoothly.

Gradually step back slowly (slow enough to barely notice) until eventually you are out of eyesight or hearing distance.

Scenario 5

AN INVITATION TO DINNER AT YOUR EXCEPTIONALLY TALKATIVE AUNT AND UNCLE'S HOUSE

"I'm on a cleanse."

Specify that you can't have sugar, dairy, bread, alcohol, meat, vegetables, or whatever else they would be serving.

"My psychic suggested I avoid dinners that
aren't at home for a while."

Pick a new volunteer opportunity and start volunteering on that date.

At least you are avoiding for a good cause.

Scenario 6

HAVING HOUSEGUESTS
WHO ARE DEFINITELY EXTROVERTS

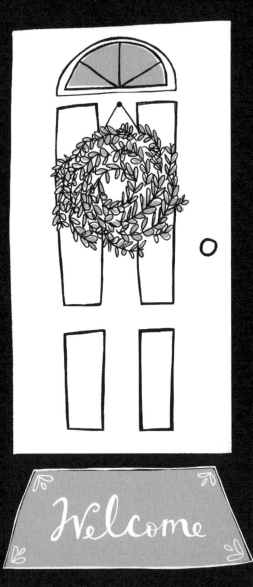

Arrange daily itineraries of activities for them during their stay.

Pack them lunches and send them off to explore anywhere but your house.

Treat your guests to a hotel room.

They don't need to know that
it's really a treat for yourself.

Stash some necessities in your room.

Pick things that can sustain you if you need to take a break for a few hours in solitude.

Chapter 3

COWORKERS

How to avoid spending extra time with colleagues

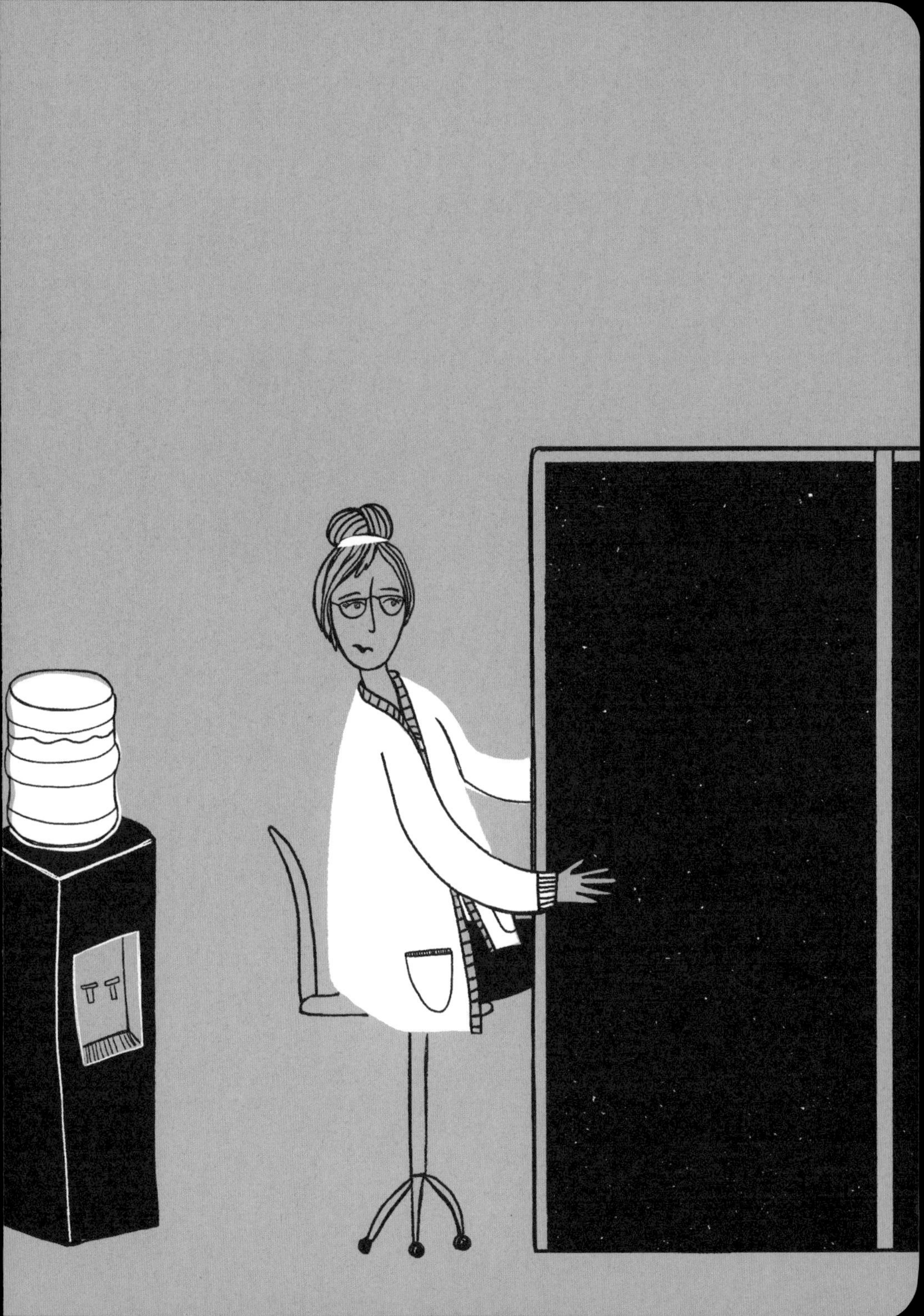

Scenario 1

AN INVITATION TO JOIN IN ON SOME AFTER-WORK KARAOKE

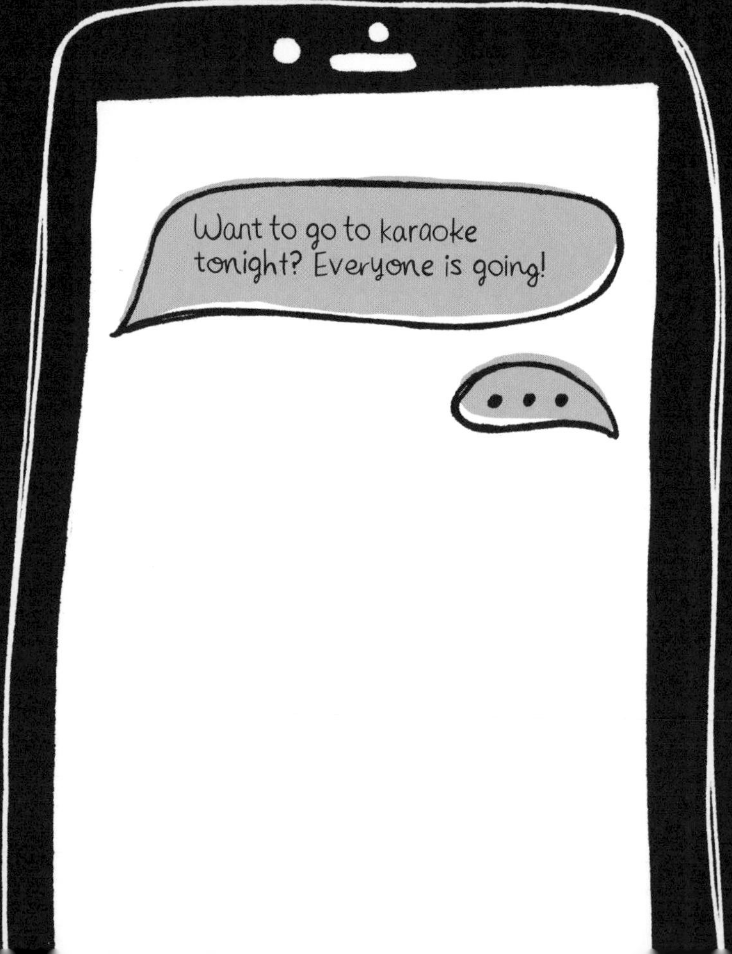
Want to go to karaoke tonight? Everyone is going!
...

"I'd love to, but I have book club."

(Who has to know it's with yourself?)

"My friend is recovering from_____,
so I'm bringing her_____."

Mix and match with whatever
ailment your "friend" has.

"aerobics, kickboxing, cooking, etc."

"I already prepaid for a(n) _____ class tonight. Otherwise I totally would!"

Scenario 2

YOUR CHATTY COWORKERS LIKE EATING LUNCH AS A GROUP

Pack odoriferous food
for lunch for a while.

An adventurous palate is required.

Play detective and find out
where everyone doesn't like to go.
Insist on always going there.

Eventually, you may be conveniently not invited.

Use lunchtime to run errands.

Keep a to-do list on you in case evidence is needed.

Scenario 3

ENTERING THE BREAK ROOM IS LIKE WALKING INTO A CHITCHAT TRAP

Develop a habit of accidentally blabbing TV or movie spoilers.

Be careful because loss of popularity may ensue.

Carry and read a book at all times
when not at your desk.

Tip:
Use a business book
to look absorbed
in your work.

Secretly post an official-looking "Quiet Zone" sign in the room.

Stealthily repost when necessary.

Scenario 4

RUNNING INTO SOMEONE WHO LIKES MAKING SMALL TALK IN THE RESTROOM

Forward something lengthy and
distracting to coworkers immediately prior
to going to the restroom.

Pick intriguing clickbait to buy yourself some time.

Tip: Mention that you spilled something if you sense any lingering suspicion.

Grab a paper towel and leave.

Return later and try again.

"Oh, I think ______ is looking for you."

Tip:

Name someone with whom you have prior approval to act as your diversion.

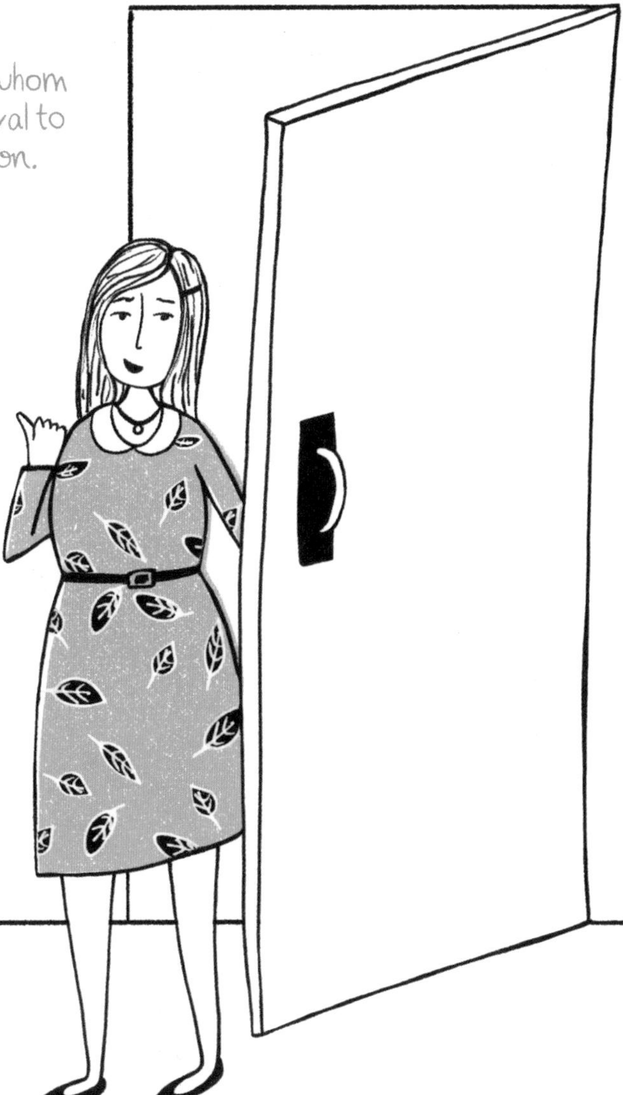

ARRIVING AT WORK AND WALKING IN AT THE SAME TIME AS YOUR CHATTY COLLEAGUE

Pause and "look" for something
very, very hard to find in your bag.

You'll find it as soon as there is enough space between you two.

Do some seated yoga stretches in your car.

Keep stretching until that coworker has safely entered the building.

Answer a phone call.

Or at least look like you are.

Scenario 6

A NETWORKING EVENT THAT REQUIRES SOME MINGLING

Volunteer with setup and other small tasks during the event.

Staying busy reduces awkward hovering.

Get physical evidence that you attended by appearing in at least one photo that will likely be shared online.

This protects reputation and will give the illusion that you are a mingler at ease and an active participant in your community (even if you were technically only present for 10 minutes).

Attend the event with an
extrovert buddy who understands you.

Ideally, this is someone who doesn't mind doing all of the talking.

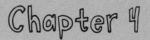

Chapter 4

ACQUAINTANCES

How to avoid any awkward
acknowledgment of recognition

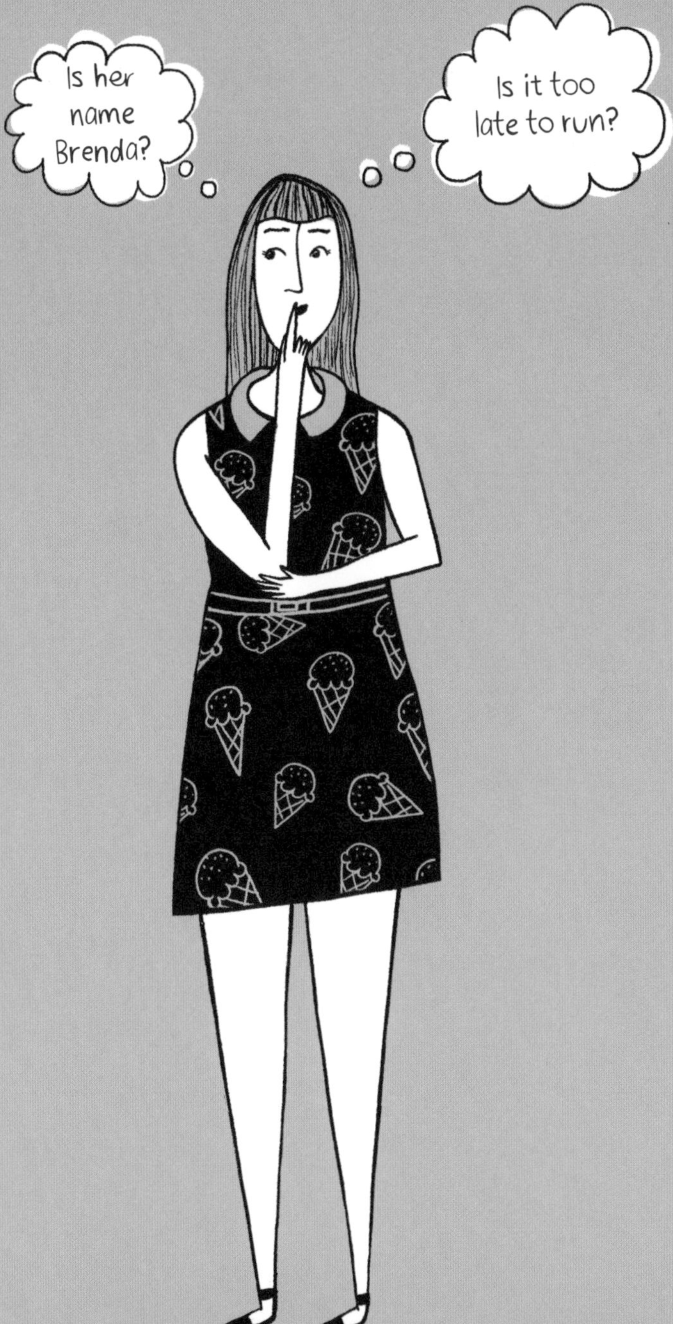
Is her name Brenda?
Is it too late to run?

ATTENDING A PARTY YOUR FRIEND INVITED YOU TO AND ONLY KNOWING HER

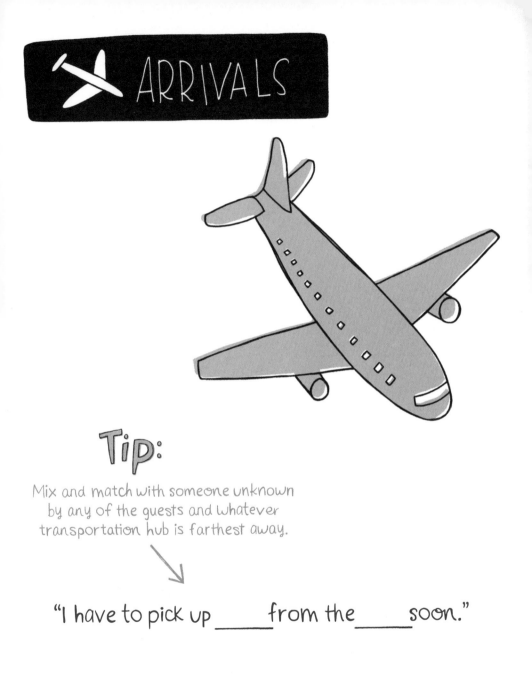

ARRIVALS

Tip:

Mix and match with someone unknown by any of the guests and whatever transportation hub is farthest away.

"I have to pick up ____ from the ____ soon."

"I forgot _____ in my car! Be right back."

Go on a self-guided tour of the home,
right out another door.

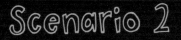

Scenario 2

RUNNING INTO SOMEONE YOU KNOW FROM ONLINE WHILE OUT SHOPPING AT THE GROCERY STORE

Put on some earbuds.

Music is optional.

Continuously study your
shopping list intensely.

Become a loyal shopper at a
24-hour grocery store.

Avoid future encounters by only shopping after 11:00 PM.

Scenario 3

OUT SHOPPING AND SEEING A FRIEND'S COWORKER WHO YOU MET AT A PARTY A WHILE AGO

Pick up your speed and appear to be in a hurry.

Let your momentum imply that you
have no time for pleasantries.

Enter the nearest establishment immediately.

Wear your hair in a big, fluffy style
to hide your face while you are out.

Invest in extensions or wigs if necessary.

Scenario 4

YOUR NEIGHBOR LOVES TO MAKE SMALL TALK DURING YARDWORK

Announce that you have something
simmering on your stove that
needs to be checked on.

Plant tall bushes, hedges, and any plants that conveniently obstruct any potential eye contact throughout your yard.

Tip:

Cultivate your yard into a maze of private plant tunnels if you are feeling extra ambitious.

Keep noisy power equipment with you while outside.

Simply turn on at first sight of your neighbor.

Tip:
Try a Weedwacker or leaf blower!

Scenario 5

YOU NOTICE THAT THE BARTENDER IS SOMEONE YOU WENT TO HIGH SCHOOL WITH

Order a beverage large enough
to sustain you for the rest of your time
there without needing a refill.

Build your own disguise kit.

Keep it handy at all times.

Locate the dimmest area at the bar to order at.

Scenario 6

SPOTTING SOMEONE A FEW TABLES AWAY WHO YOUR ROOMMATE DATED NOT LONG AGO

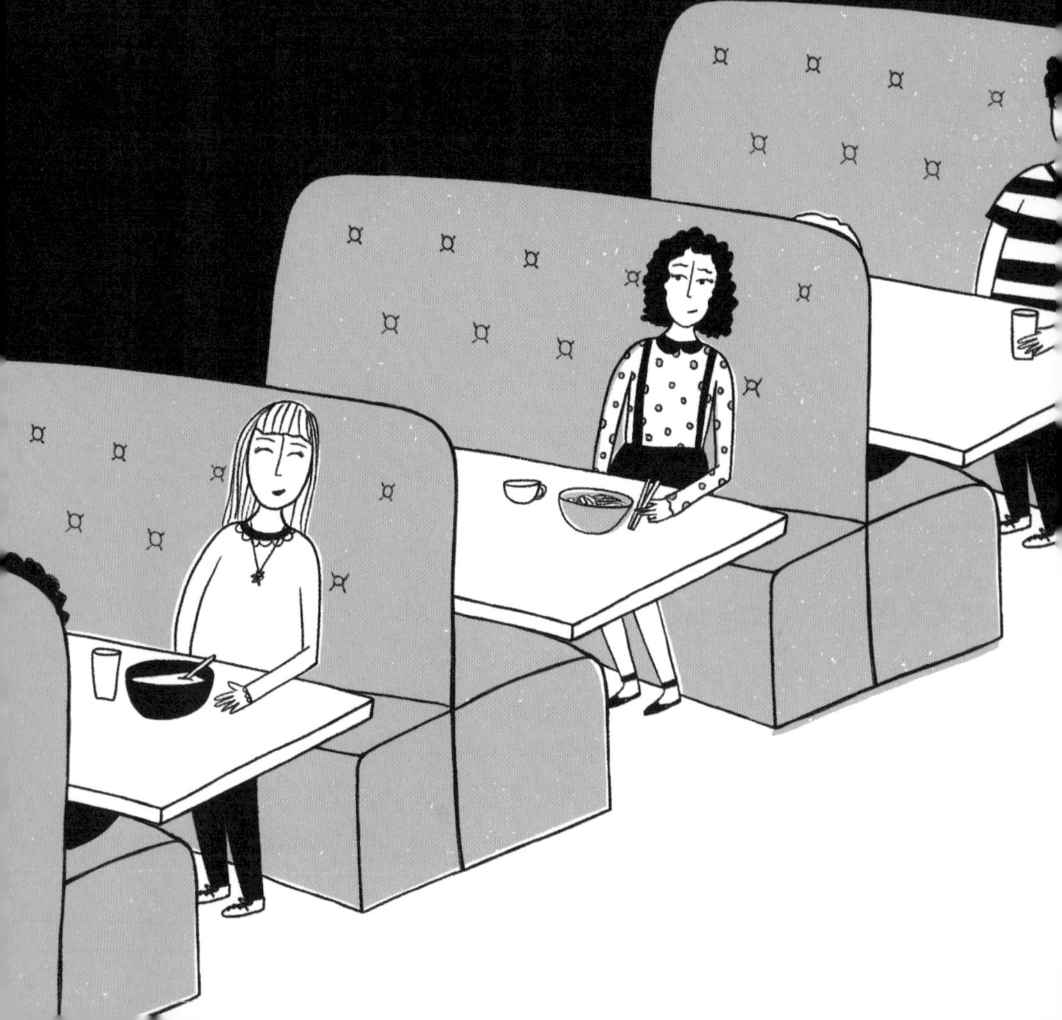

Become a fan of big, floppy hats.

Position accordingly to shield eye contact.

Order the tallest menu items possible.

Maybe you actually are in the mood for 35 pancakes, anyway.

Tip:

Eat your food ~~fortress~~ slowly if you still need more time to hide.

Keep your menu on the table after ordering.

You can browse desserts and casually conceal your face.

Chapter 5

STRANGERS

How to impede unnecessary interaction
with people you don't know

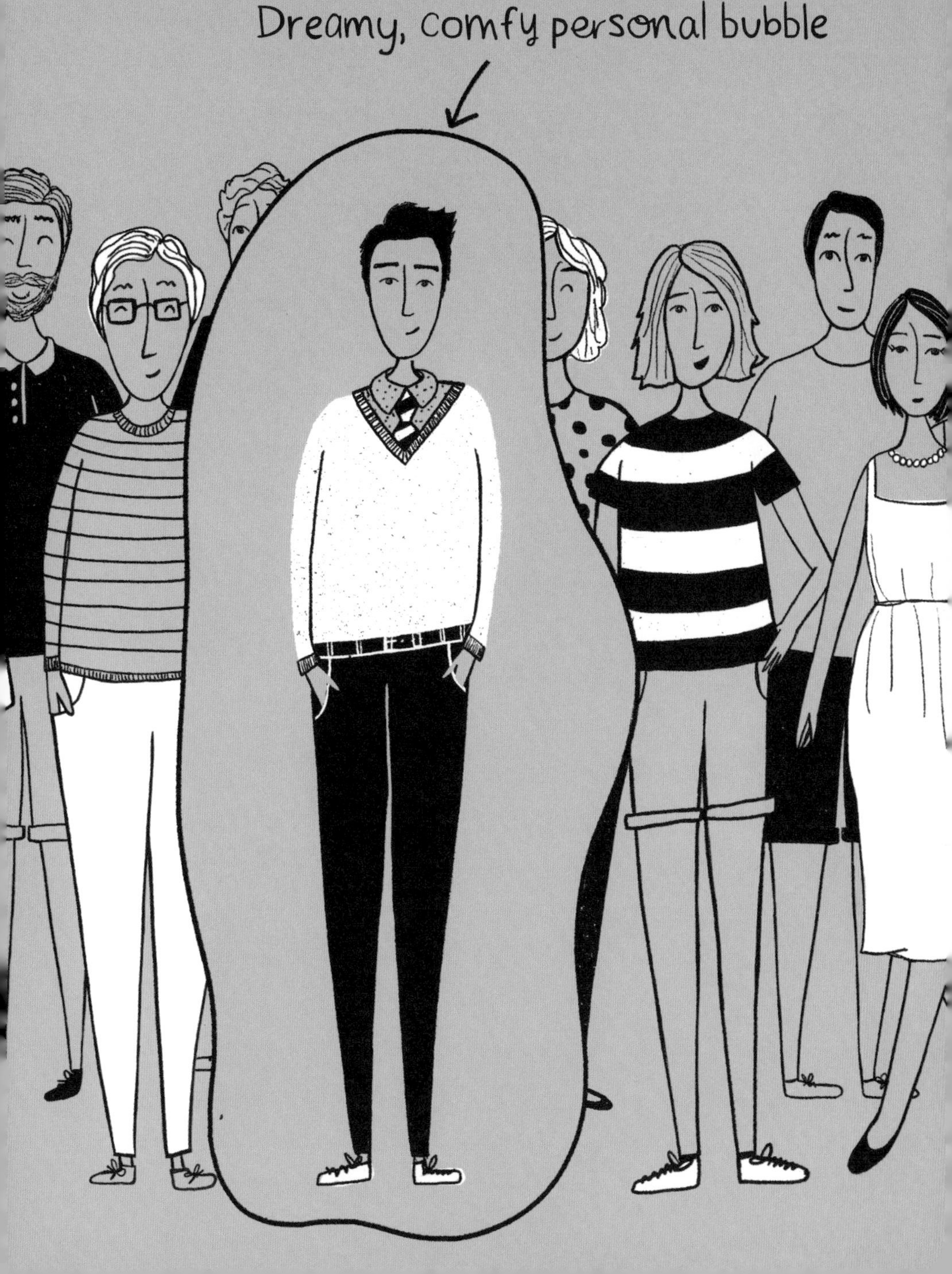
Dreamy, comfy personal bubble

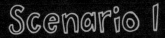

Scenario 1

BEING SANDWICHED BETWEEN MOTORMOUTH SEATMATES ON YOUR FLIGHT

Learn a few basic phrases in an obscure language to hinder any two-way communication.

You may have to sacrifice dinner or beverage service to keep the deception going (unless you can manage with body language).

Tip:

Pick a language likely to be unknown by your seatmates.

Belarusian Phrase Book

Indulge in pungent food immediately before your flight.

No mints for you!

THANK YOU!

- Cheeseburger
  - extra onions
  - garlic mayo
- Garlic Knots
- Large Coffee

Never board without a sleep mask
and bulky scarf to slink into.

Scenario 2

SHOPPING AT SMALL VENUES, LIKE CRAFT SHOW BOOTHS, WITH EAGER AND ATTENTIVE WORKERS

Tip:

Not for use on a hot day!

"My dog is waiting for me in my car."

Maybe you have a dog, maybe you don't.

Locate the least expensive item.
This will act as your ticket out of the shop.

Create space in your budget for "exit purchases" that are useful when faced with awkward shop interactions.

You

Hire a kidnapper.

Keep them on speed dial.

Scenario 3

YOUR FAVORITE PARK IS FULL OF LOQUACIOUS REGULARS

Shout "There you are!" in any direction
and walk away.

Wear head-to-toe camouflage
specific to each season.

Invest in a jet pack.

The quickest of quick evacuations.

Scenario 4

CROWDED WAITING ROOMS

Bring an interesting newspaper with you
and position directly in front
of your face, cleverly creating a shield.

Bring your own personal paging system and politely ask reception to buzz you when ready.

You can enjoy waiting in solitude outside in the meantime.

Just like in restaurants.

Borrow your dog's cone of shame
to wear temporarily.

Scenario 5

WORKING OUT AMONG MANY OUTGOING AND SOCIABLE GYM MEMBERS

Retreat safely into child's pose in yoga class.

Tip:

Perfect for waiting
for class to begin.

Take a sip of water when sensing you are about to be singled out by the instructor.

Keep sipping as long as you need to.

Sit down in a meditative pose
if you sense someone approaching.

You'll seem very in tune with the universe and yourself.

Scenario 6

STRANGERS AT YOUR DOOR WHO ARE SELLING VARIOUS PRODUCTS, RELIGIONS, ETC.

Grab your things and rush out the door, stating that you are late for a(n) _____ appointment.

You may need to make a trip around the block until they leave the premises for good.

Tip:

Increase believability by mentioning the type of appointment (dentist, chiropractor, and so on).

Place a foreboding sign on your lawn.

Swaddle something before answering the door.

"Shh...Baby is sleeping."

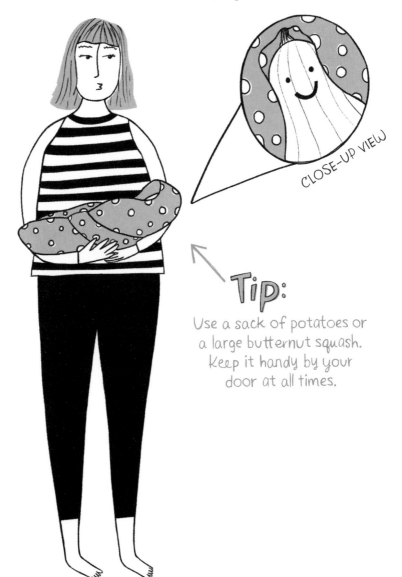

CLOSE-UP VIEW

Tip:

Use a sack of potatoes or a large butternut squash. Keep it handy by your door at all times.

Acknowledgments

I would like to thank everyone at Andrews McMeel for helping this book come alive and, more importantly, for believing in my ideas. I'm so grateful to Patty Rice, the kindest, most encouraging editor ever and whom I am very lucky to work with. Thank you to my stellar agent, Laurie Abkemeier, for your brilliant wisdom and your extraordinary intuition and ability to draw my dream projects out of me. To my dear friends who share my work and come to craft shows and events—I'm humbled by your support. Thank you for understanding and still being my friend even when I don't want to hang out. To my sister, Sarah Vaz, for always being there for me, especially with pepperoni and cheese. To my mom, Pat Vaz, who knew all along that I could do this. Thank you for all the times you've been my assistant, therapist, cheerleader, and friend all in one. Lastly, to my husband, Joby Springsteen, for your perspective and ever-thoughtful advice. Thank you for making tater tot pizzas and reminding me to shower and sleep during the busiest (and happiest) fall ever.

About the author

KATIE VAZ is an illustrator, author, hand-letterer, and graphic designer. She also designs her own line of greeting cards, prints, and other stationery products, which are sold both online and in brick-and-mortar shops across North America. Her cards capture the sticky sweet, awkward but funny, sometimes emotionally heavy things that need to be said in all types of relationships. Katie is the author of *Don't Worry, Eat Cake: A Coloring Book to Help You Feel a Little Bit Better about Everything* and *Make Yourself Cozy: A Guide for Practicing Self-Care*. Katie also works as a freelance illustrator and designer on a variety of branding, illustration, print, and packaging projects. Her work has been featured online at BuzzFeed, *Real Simple, Woman's Day*, and POPSUGAR and in *Time Out New York* magazine. She studied graphic design (BFA) at the Rochester Institute of Technology in Rochester, New York, and integrated design (MA) at Anhalt University of Applied Sciences in Dessau, Germany. She lives in upstate New York and online at www.katievaz.com.

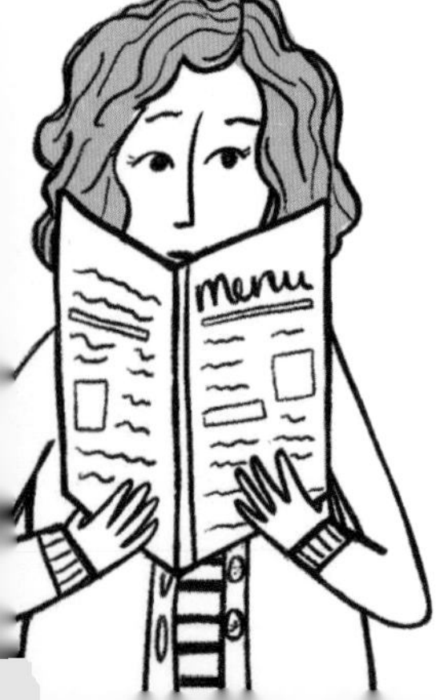
menu